Extreme Habitats

Ocean
Survival

Susie Hodge

Consultant: Jean-luc Solandt, Marine Conservation Society

 **Gareth Stevens**
Publishing

Please visit our web site at: **www.garethstevens.com**
For a free color catalog describing **Gareth Stevens Publishing's** list of high-quality books,
call 1-800-542-2595 (USA) or 1-800-387-3178 (Canada).
Gareth Stevens Publishing's fax: 1-877-542-2596

Library of Congress Cataloging-in-Publication Data

Hodge, Susie.
   Ocean survival / Susie Hodge. — North American ed.
     p. cm. — (Extreme habitats)
   Includes index.
   ISBN-10: 0-8368-8247-4   ISBN-13: 978-0-8368-8247-6 (lib. bdg.)
   1. Marine ecology—Juvenile literature. I. Title.
  QH541.5.S3H58   2007
  551.46—dc22   2007015842

This North American edition first published in 2008 by
Gareth Stevens Publishing
A Weekly Reader® Company
1 Reader's Digest Road
Pleasantville, NY 10570-7000 USA

This U.S. edition copyright © 2008 by Gareth Stevens, Inc.
Original edition copyright © ticktock Entertainment Ltd 2007
First published in Great Britain in 2007 by ticktock Media Ltd.,
Unit 2, Orchard Business Centre, North Farm Road,
Tunbridge Wells, Kent, TN2 3XF, United Kingdom

Ticktock project editor: Rebecca Clunes
Ticktock project designer: Sara Greasley

Gareth Stevens managing editor: Valerie J. Weber
Gareth Stevens editor: Tea Benduhn
Gareth Stevens art direction: Tammy West
Gareth Stevens graphic designer: Dave Kowalski
Gareth Stevens production: Jessica Yanke

Photo credits: (t=top, b=bottom, l=left, r=right, c=center)
Shane Anderson/NOAA 27b; Getty Tobias Bernhard/Getty 10b; Bettman/Corbis 8l; Brandon D. Cole/Corbis 17tl; Corbis Lawrence
Manning/Corbis 5b; Cousteau Society/Getty 12b; Mike Watson Images/SuperStock 1; NASA 13cr; National Undersea Research Program
OAR/NURP/Woods Hole Oceanographic Inst 8r; Flip Nicklin/Minden Pictures/FLPA 20b; NOAA 5c, 9tl, 29bl; Pierre Perrin/Corbis Sygma 25t,
25ct; Matthew Polak/Corbis Sygma 28; Bruce Robison/Corbis 16b; D. Weaver/FGBNMS 9cl; Doc White/naturepl.com 16t; Norbert
Wu/Getty 16–17; Oxford Scientific 21b; Shutterstock 4–5, 6c, 6–7b, 7r, 9cr, 10–11,10t, 11t, 13cl, 17tr, 17b, 18t, 18–19, 19t, 19cr, 20t, 21t,
21ct, 21cb, 22–23 (all), 24r, 24l, 25cb, 25b, 26t, 26b, 27t, 27cr, 27cb, 31; Ticktock Media Archive 5t, 6t, 11b, 18b; VideoRay 29tr. All artwork
Ticktock Media Archive except 4 and 13t Cosmographics. Front cover Oxford Scientific; back cover Shutterstock.

Every effort has been made to trace the copyright holders for the photos used in this book. The publisher apologizes,
in advance, for any unintentional omissions and would be pleased to insert the appropriate acknowledgements in any
subsequent edition of this publication.

Printed in the United States of America

2 3 4 5 6 7 8 9 11 10 09 08

Contents

Words that appear in the glossary are printed in **boldface**
type the first time they occur in the text.

The Blue Planet

This map shows the world's five oceans.

Oceans are enormous! They are thousands of miles (kilometers) wide and cover 72 percent of Earth's surface. All that water looks blue from a distance, which is why some scientists call Earth the Blue Planet.

The world under water is more extreme than anything on land. Oceans contain the tallest mountains and the deepest valleys on the planet.

Oceans affect Earth's temperatures. The water absorbs warmth from the Sun. Constantly moving **currents** spread this heat around the globe, warming the air above them and the land around them.

The crown-of-thorns starfish is found in the Pacific and Indian Oceans. Its spines protect it from predators.

Strange creatures and plants live in the oceans. Some live on the **seabed**, while others spend their lives near the surface. Living in water is completely different from living on land. Ocean animals and plants have special ways of surviving in their underwater world.

Some fish swim in big groups called shoals.

OCEAN SURVIVAL TIPS

Diving deep can change how well the human brain works. Some divers are not able to think clearly when swimming in deep water. When you dive, be sure to bring an air tank to keep your brain working well.

Going Diving

The sea lily is an animal, but it is often mistaken for a plant.

Warm, shallow waters are often full of life and very colorful. Sunlight never reaches deeper waters, however, so the bottom of the ocean is cold and dark.

The underwater world is beautiful to swim in. Diving is dangerous, however, even with modern equipment. If you are going under water, be prepared!

All animals need **oxygen** to live. Fish take in oxygen from the water that moves over their **gills.** People get oxygen from the air, so divers must bring their own air with them. Without air, you would quickly lose consciousness, and you would die in minutes.

Queen angelfish live in shallow, warm waters.

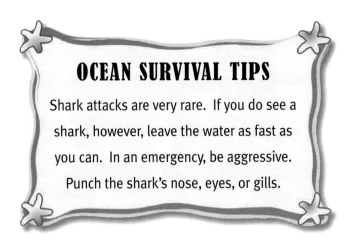

OCEAN SURVIVAL TIPS

Shark attacks are very rare. If you do see a shark, however, leave the water as fast as you can. In an emergency, be aggressive. Punch the shark's nose, eyes, or gills.

When divers return to the surface after a deep dive, tiny bubbles of **nitrogen** can form in their blood. This condition, called the **bends**, is dangerous and very painful. Sometimes, the nitrogen bubbles can kill a person. To avoid the bends, divers surface slowly or go into a **decompression chamber.**

A scuba diver takes a photo of a coral reef.

OCEAN NOTEBOOK

How do you explore the oceans? It depends on how deep you want to go!

- Trained divers can hold their breath and swim down to 100 feet (30 m).

- Scuba divers breathe from tanks of air strapped to their backs. They can dive 165 feet (50 m) down.

- To reach depths of up to 1,970 feet (600 m), divers wear a hard diving suit that is as solid and sturdy as a one-person submarine.

Most submarines can dive to at least 820 feet (250 m).

- For underwater research, scientists use a type of submarine called a submersible. Most submersibles cannot dive deeper than about 14,765 feet (4,500 m) underwater.

7

Challenger Deep is far away from any landmass.

The Deepest Place on Earth

The ocean floor is not flat. It has enormous mountains and deep valleys. The deepest known point on Earth is in the Marianas Trench under the Pacific Ocean. Known as Challenger Deep, the deepest point is about 7 miles (11 kilometers) below the ocean's surface.

At the bottom of Challenger Deep, the water pressure is enormous. If you were to dive that deeply, you would feel as if you were being crushed under the weight of fifty jumbo jets. The pressure, the cold, and the dark make life seem impossible at such depths.

More than forty years ago, however, scientists built a submersible, called *Trieste*, that could reach the bottom of Challenger Deep. In 1960, *Trieste* took five hours to travel down. It spent twenty minutes at the bottom and traveled back up in about three hours.

Trieste is being lifted out of the water. It is now at the Navy Museum in Washington, D.C.

Before *Trieste*'s journey, scientists believed nothing could live below 1 mile (1.6 km) down. The scientists onboard *Trieste* were amazed to discover that some animals and plants actually live in the crushing black depths.

Scientists use special equipment to make maps of the sea floor.

Today's scientists use the submarine Alvin to explore the ocean depths.

Today, no submersible is able to go to the bottom of Challenger Deep. A submersible known as *Alvin* can dive down almost 3 miles (5 km), which is the deepest any can go.

This photo was taken by Alvin deep in the Hudson Bay canyon off the coast of Canada.

OCEAN SURVIVAL TIPS

If you are taking a trip aboard *Alvin*, check the weather. If it is too windy or the waves are too high, it could be too dangerous to launch *Alvin*. Your trip will be delayed until the weather improves.

OCEAN NOTEBOOK

Scientists divide the ocean depths into different zones.

- Sunlight zone — from the ocean surface down to about 656 feet (200 m). Most sea creatures live in this zone.

Most ocean life stays in the sunlight zone. This zone is the only one where enough light shines for plants to grow.

- Twilight zone — the area between 660 feet (200 m) and 3,280 feet (1,000 m). Some light reaches here.

- Midnight zone — from 3,280 feet (1,000 m) to 19,690 feet (6,000 m). This zone is freezing cold and completely dark. It usually extends to the ocean floor.

- Deepest ocean — the trenches in the ocean floor below 19,690 feet (6,000 m). Very little is known about these remote areas.

The Coldest Oceans

The two coldest seas are the Arctic Ocean and the Southern Ocean. Thick ice floats on top of the Arctic Ocean, covering most of the area. The Southern Ocean surrounds the continent of Antarctica.

Gentoo penguins live near Antarctica. They dive as many as 450 times each day in search of food.

The Southern Ocean is colder than the Arctic Ocean. Currents and winds block warm air and water from entering it. Warm currents from the Atlantic and Pacific Oceans flow into the Arctic Ocean, however.

Each polar ocean freezes over during its winter. From April to September, thick ice covers 6 million square miles (16 million square kilometers) of the Arctic Ocean. From October to March, ice covers 7 million square miles (18 million sq km) of the Southern Ocean.

When the ice sheets melt in summer, each ocean is filled with **icebergs**. About 10 percent of an iceberg floats above water. These giant chunks of ice can cause great damage to ships.

A diver swims between two icebergs in the Southern Ocean.

OCEAN NOTEBOOK

- A range of **marine** life can be found in the Arctic and Southern Oceans, including whales, sharks, jellyfish, squid, crabs, ice fish, and seals.

Beluga whales are white. Their color camouflages them in the icy Arctic Ocean.

- Polar bears live in the Arctic. They swim from iceberg to iceberg looking for seals to eat. Webbing between their toes helps them swim.

- Penguins live near the Southern Ocean. Emperor penguins can dive down to depths of 660 feet (200 m) and stay under water for twenty minutes while they hunt for fish.

OCEAN SURVIVAL TIPS

If you are diving in polar oceans, wear a very thick **dry suit** to keep warm. Some divers also wear a harness with a rope. You can use the rope to tie yourself to the surface so you will not get trapped under the ice.

The Largest Ocean

Equator

The dark blue areas show where water is coldest in the Pacific Ocean.

The Pacific Ocean is bigger than the other four oceans put together. It covers a larger area of Earth than all the land does. It is so huge that, when looking at Earth from outer space, one viewpoint shows no land at all — only the Pacific Ocean!

The Pacific has a greater range of temperatures than any other ocean. Near the **equator**, water temperatures are about 86 °Fahrenheit (30 °Celsius). Temperatures in the far south of the Pacific, near the Southern Ocean, are near freezing.

The Pacific Ocean contains less salt around the equator than it does elsewhere. Rainstorms, which bring fresh water to the ocean, are more frequent near the equator. Enough freshwater falls to make this part of the ocean less salty!

Divers examine an underwater volcano in French Polynesia in the Pacific Ocean. Volcanoes formed most of the islands in this region.

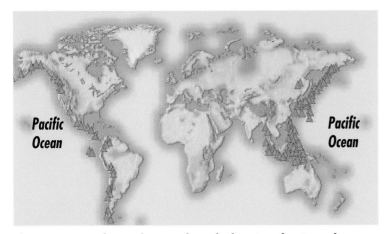

The orange triangles on the map show the location of active volcanoes around the Pacific Ocean.

More than 80 percent of the world's active volcanoes are in the Pacific Ocean. Most of them are near the land around the edges of the ocean. Some people call these volcanic areas the Ring of Fire.

*Clownfish are among the many colorful **species** of fish living in the Pacific Ocean. They can be found along the coast of Southeast Asia.*

OCEAN SURVIVAL TIPS

The beaked sea snake lives in shallow waters in the Pacific and Indian Oceans. Its bite is deadly. If you are bitten by a sea snake, get medical help immediately!

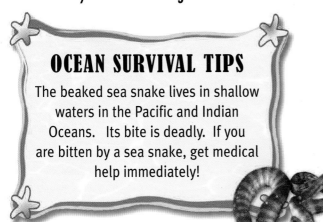

OCEAN NOTEBOOK

- The Pacific Ocean is often swept by huge storms called cyclones. In the Atlantic Ocean, these storms are called hurricanes.

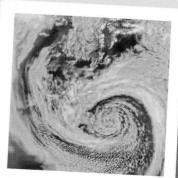

A cyclone crosses the Pacific Ocean and heads toward Alaska.

- Hurricanes and cyclones travel at speeds between 100 and 200 miles (160 and 320 km) per hour. They can stretch up to 590 miles (950 km) across.

- The continents are constantly moving. South America, for example, is moving west by a few inches (centimeters) every year. The Pacific Ocean, therefore, is slowly getting smaller.

The Moving Seas

*The oceans are always moving. Winds blow waves across the surface of the water. Currents carry huge amounts of water deep beneath the surface. **Tides** move in and out with Earth's **rotation**. **Tsunamis** sweep across coastlines.*

A massive underwater earthquake in 2004 caused tsunamis in countries bordering the Indian Ocean.

The Sun heats the water near the equator. Warm currents near the ocean's surface flow from the equator toward the poles. The currents bring warm weather to the areas along the way. Cold water from the poles sinks down. The water cools the areas along the way to the equator. Other forces can make the ocean waters move, too.

Many waves are created by winds. Stronger winds make bigger waves.

Underwater earthquakes and volcanic eruptions can shake the ocean with tremendous force. They generate huge waves called tsunamis. These massive columns of water rise up from the sea floor and surge across long distances at speeds as fast as 500 miles (800 km) per hour.

When a tsunami reaches shallow coastal waters, it can rise up to 130 feet (40 m) high. That is about as tall as a twelve-story building! The waves crash into shore with enormous force and can destroy whole towns, killing thousands of people.

Monsters of the Deep

Far beneath the ocean's surface, the world is dark and cold, with water pressure strong enough to crush a bowling ball. Few creatures live in these depths. The animals that do survive here fight hard for their food. They are some of the ocean's deadliest hunters.

Viper fish have long fangs. When they bite into their prey, there is little chance of escape.

Like many fish living in darkness, the viper fish can make its own light. It has a row of organs along the side of its body that can produce light, which it uses as a **lure**. When other fish swim toward the lights, the viper fish attacks!

The fangtooth fish lives as far down as 16,400 feet (5,000 m) below the surface. During the day, it usually stays in the deepest water where it is safe from predators. At night, it swims upward to hunt smaller fish and squid.

Hagfish live more than 3,280 feet (1,000 m) below the surface. They bury themselves inside the

Although the adult fangtooth looks scary, it probably will not hurt you. It is only 6 inches (16 cm) long!

Young fangtooth fish like this look very different from the adults. Scientists once thought they were two different species.

Hagfish produce a sticky slime to protect themselves from predators. The slime covers the predator's gills, so it cannot breathe.

bodies of other fish. Then they eat their victims from the inside out!

The giant squid lives about 6,560 feet (2,000 m) below the surface. It is one of the world's largest animals, growing up to 40 feet (12 m) long. Only one adult giant squid has ever been caught alive. Many other squid have been found, however, inside the stomachs of whales.

OCEAN SURVIVAL TIPS

Squid can be found at every depth of the ocean. A squid has a bony beak that it could use to bite a diver and cause injury. Squid bites are very rare, but if you do see a squid, watch out!

The Most Colorful Oceans

The oceans around coral reefs are full of color. Coral reefs form in warm, shallow waters, which are often near **tropical** countries. One coral reef may be home to as many as three thousand species of living creatures.

This lined butterfly fish will chase away other butterfly fish that swim into its part of the coral reef.

Coral reefs are formed by tiny animals called polyps. Polyps use minerals in the sea to make protective outer skeletons. When a polyp dies, its skeleton helps form a coral reef. New polyps attach themselves to the skeletons, adding a new layer to the reef. Polyps form coral reefs at about the same rate as your fingernails grow!

Many sea turtles live near coral reefs.

The Great Barrier Reef is in the Indian Ocean near Australia. At 90 miles (150 km) wide and more than 1,240 miles (2,000 km) long, it is the world's biggest coral reef.

This red coral is growing on rocks in the Pacific Ocean near Indonesia.

Brightly colored fish and thousands of other sea creatures live in the shelter of coral reefs.

Thousands of species of fish live in coral reefs. Many of them, such as angelfish, clownfish, and parrotfish, have bright colors and bold markings.

OCEAN SURVIVAL TIPS

A single sea wasp has enough poison to kill fifty people. These jellyfish are very hard to see in the water. If you swim near the Great Barrier Reef, check the beaches for warning signs.

OCEAN NOTEBOOK

- There are many different types of coral. Rose coral looks like roses, and sea fan coral resembles little fans. Brain coral looks like a human brain!

- Coral often grows on the wrecks of sunken ships and planes.

- To prevent getting swept away by currents, sea horses twist their tails around coral to anchor themselves. If they see a predator, they change color to match their surroundings.

Sea horses are a type of fish. They range in size from 2 inches (5 centimeters) to 12 inches (30 cm).

- Many fish hide in coral during the day and come out at night to feed. Others hide at night and feed in the daytime!

FACT FILE:

Ocean Plants

*Plants need warmth, light, and the right balance of minerals to grow. Oceans are an ideal place for many plants to live. Plants range in size from tiny **phytoplankton** to enormous seaweeds.*

Seaweeds often have hollow bumps on their stems. These air-filled pockets help them float in the water.

- Some plants do not have roots or anchors, and they drift along in ocean currents.

- Phytoplankton is made up of billions of tiny plants, floating together in the ocean.

- Creatures that eat phytoplankton are then eaten by other animals.

- Vast forests of giant seaweeds, known as kelp, grow in oceans.

- Kelp attaches itself to the ocean floor with rootlike anchors called holdfasts. Many fish eat kelp, and others hunt for prey hidden in it.

- Kelp is the largest of all ocean plants. Some kelp can grow to nearly 200 feet (60 m) high.

- Near California, kelp grows as fast as about 24 inches (60 cm) a day!

Kelp plants form the forests of the sea.

Animals That Look Like Plants

- **Sea anemones**
  - Sea anemones look like bright, underwater flowers.
  - They can move small distances by sliding slowly.
  - Their "petals" are actually tentacles that sting any creature that gets too close.

Sea anemones

- **Sea urchins**
  - Sea urchins grow up to 4 inches (10 cm) wide.
  - They are small, round creatures covered with spines.
  - A sea urchin's mouth is at the bottom of its body, and it scrapes **algae** off rocks for food.

Sea urchin

- **Sponges**
  - Sponges live at all ocean depths. The sponges in shallow waters are often brightly colored.
  - They cannot move, and they do not have eyes or mouths.
  - They eat by drawing water in through their skin and collecting tiny bits of food from the water.

Sea sponge

- Sea grasses look like ordinary grass. They grow on shallow, sandy seabeds often next to coral reefs.

- Manatees are sometimes known as sea cows. They graze on sea grass, just as cows do on land!

Manatees are slow-moving, gentle mammals that spend large parts of their days grazing on sea plants.

FACT FILE:

Ocean Animals

At least fifteen thousand species of fish live in the ocean. Other animals include lobsters, shrimp, squid, worms, jellyfish, and tiny microscopic creatures.

The fugu is poisonous. It is also known as a blowfish, swellfish, globefish, or puffer fish because it can puff up its body so much that a predator cannot swallow it.

- About 80 percent of the world's fish live in the oceans.

- Sharks are a type of fish. There are more than 350 species of sharks.

- Sharks have a good sense of sight and of smell. They are among the deadliest hunters in the ocean.

- At just 9 inches (22 cm) long, the pygmy shark is the world's smallest shark. It lives in warm oceans.

- In the darkest zones of the ocean, many animals create light by mixing chemicals inside their bodies.

- The light produced by most sea animals is blue-green since this color can be seen best in water.

- Some creatures give off light constantly. Others flash their lights on and off.

The Pacific cleaner shrimp lives on coral reefs in the Pacific and Indian Oceans.

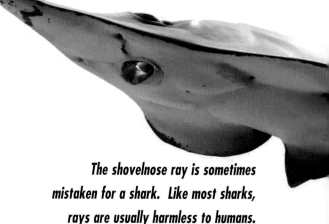

The shovelnose ray is sometimes mistaken for a shark. Like most sharks, rays are usually harmless to humans.

Other Sea Animals

- **Mammals**
  - Seals, walruses, and sea lions are mammals that spend most of their lives in water.
  - Although they look like fish, whales and dolphins are mammals. Like all mammals, whales and dolphins breathe air and feed their young on milk.

Dolphin

- **Birds**
  - Penguins have flippers and webbed feet. They swim very fast under water, twisting and turning to catch fish.
  - The wandering albatross is the biggest seabird. It spends all of its life at sea, only coming to land to nest.

Wandering albatross

- **Reptiles**
  - The saltwater crocodile can grow up to 26 feet (8 m) long. It is found in waters near Australia, and it can swim far distances from land.
  - Some snakes and turtles also live in the sea.

Saltwater crocodile

- The anglerfish uses a light over its head as a lure. When small fish move toward the attractive light, the anglerfish swallows them.

WHY DO SOME SEA ANIMALS PRODUCE LIGHT?	
SEA ANIMAL	**USE OF LIGHT**
JELLYFISH	AS A WARNING TO STAY AWAY
SQUID	AS CAMOUFLAGE
LOOSEJAW FISH	TO NAVIGATE
OSTRACOD (TINY SHRIMPLIKE CREATURES)	TO COMMUNICATE
ANGLERFISH	TO TRAP PREY

23

FACT FILE:

Ocean People

*For centuries, people have lived on or near the oceans, earning their living through fishing, shipping **cargo**, and buying and selling goods.*

In the past, spices such as pepper were valuable cargo for European sailors.

A traditional fishing boat sails near Tanzania.

- The first boats were simple rafts and canoes. In villages all over the world, people still use small boats to catch fish using traditional methods.

- Sailors in ancient times were often good at finding their way across huge distances using only the simplest equipment.

- Between the fifteenth and eighteenth centuries, European traders sailed to Asia. They brought back gold, silver, tea, gems, cotton, and silk.

- Today, ships carry 90 percent of all international goods.

- Half of the world's population lives within 125 miles (200 km) of a coast.

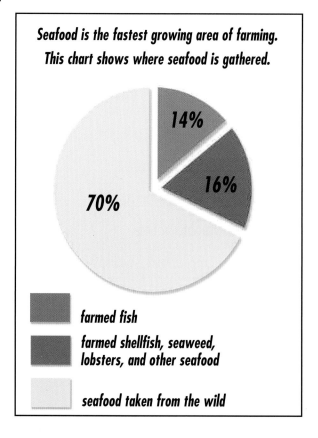

Seafood is the fastest growing area of farming. This chart shows where seafood is gathered.

14%

16%

70%

■ farmed fish

■ farmed shellfish, seaweed, lobsters, and other seafood

□ seafood taken from the wild

24

The Moken People

- **Moken seasons**
  - The Moken people, or sea gypsies, of Thailand and Malaysia spend seven or eight months of every year in their boats.
  - They go ashore during the **monsoon** season and live in simple huts, repairing their boats. During this time, they still go out to fish when they can.

A Moken man catches a turtle.

- **Boats**
  - Each boat holds one family.
  - Families sometimes dry fish on the roofs of their boats.

Moken boats

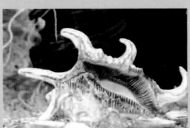

- **Trading**
  - The Moken people use nets, traps, and spears to gather fish, shells, lobsters, and other things from the sea that they can use or sell.
  - For the few months that they are ashore, the Moken people trade their ocean goods to buy rice, cooking utensils, oil, nets, and fuel.

They collect pretty shells to sell.

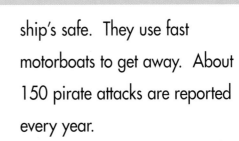

- Pirates are people who rob ships at sea. They usually work in small groups to attack cargo ships, taking all the money from the ship's safe. They use fast motorboats to get away. About 150 pirate attacks are reported every year.

Cargo ships move slowly and have few crew members. These factors make it easy for pirates to attack cargo ships.

FACT FILE:

How We Use Oceans

The oceans have always provided people with food and a means of transportation. Today, the seas are as valuable to us as ever. Companies drill for oil deep under the ocean floor, and many people use the seas for recreational activities.

People use mineral-rich sea salts in their bathwater.

- In some oceans, people farm seaweed and sell it for food or fertilizer. It is also used for making shampoo and ice cream.

- People farm salt in the shallow ocean waters near the coasts.

Seaweed can be used as a thickener in toothpastes.

- Telephone and electric companies lay cables under water. They place the cables in steel tubes to stop sharks from chewing through them.

- Telephone and electric cables are thousands of miles (km) long. Some ships are specially designed for carrying the coiled cables.

COMPARING THE WORLD'S OCEANS

OCEAN	AREA MILLIONS OF SQUARE MILES (SQ KM)	AVERAGE DEPTH MILES (KM)
PACIFIC OCEAN	39.9 (103.3)	2 (4)
ATLANTIC OCEAN	20.8 (53.8)	2 (4)
INDIAN OCEAN	17.6 (45.6)	2 (4)
SOUTHERN OCEAN	4.9 (12.6)	2 – 3 (4 – 5)
ARCTIC OCEAN	3.2 (8.2)	0.6 (1)

Fishing Boats

- **Trawlers**
  - To catch fish, trawlers drag (or trawl) heavy nets through the water or along the seabed.
  - Modern trawlers stay out at sea for weeks. They catch many species of fish, including cod, haddock, flounder, and hake.
  - The crew freezes the fish for processing later.

Trawler

- **Seiners**
  - **Seiners** target open-water fish, such as mackerel and herring.
  - They drop the net down into the water and let shoals of fish swim in. Then they close the net and haul it aboard.

Seiner

- **Long Liners**
  - These boats have long lines with baited hooks.
  - The lines can be 4,920 feet (1,500 m) in length.
  - Long liners can catch fish near the surface, such as tuna, or fish that live near the seabed, such as cod.

Long liner

- Ocean oil rigs drill under the seabed for oil and pump it out to be processed on land. One-fifth of the oil we use is pumped out from beneath the seabed.

- Some **archaeologists** spend their lives hunting for and uncovering shipwrecks. The objects they find can help them learn about the past.

Oil rigs can be attached to the ocean floor or float on the surface of the water.

FACT FILE:

Oceans in Danger

*In modern times, human activity has greatly increased ocean **pollution**. The commonest forms of pollution in the seas are waste from businesses and human **sewage**.*

Oil spills are a danger to birds, fish, and plants. A habitat can take many years to recover after an oil spill.

- Rain and rivers wash chemicals from factories and farms into oceans.

- Litter is a form of pollution.

- Oil spills are usually caused by large ocean tankers that crash at sea. The oil floats on the sea's surface, forming an oil slick that can be fatal to many marine species.

- Excessive hunting and fishing are putting some species in danger of **extinction**.

- The ocean food chain to the right shows how each type of animal relies on another for food. When pollution enters the food chain, it builds up and causes the most harm to the creatures at the top.

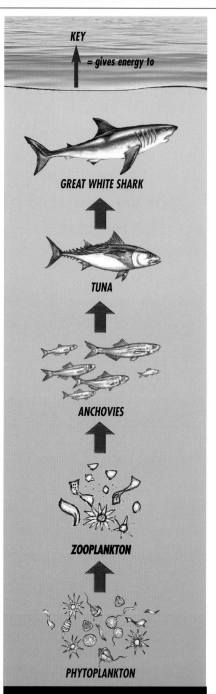

KEY

= gives energy to

GREAT WHITE SHARK

TUNA

ANCHOVIES

ZOOPLANKTON

PHYTOPLANKTON

OCEAN FOOD CHAIN

This simple food chain shows how larger creatures depend on smaller creatures for their food. If pollution affects one link in the chain, it can damage many other animals.

Positive Signs

- **Protecting the fish**
  - Many countries have introduced fishing quotas, which limit the amount of fish that people and companies can take from the sea.
  - Special nets now allow unwanted fish and dolphins to escape instead of being killed with the rest of the catch.
  - The demand for fish is high. Carefully run fish farms can help meet that demand.

Fish farm

- **Tourism**
  - People take boat trips to see whales and dolphins.
  - Diving expeditions are now very popular.

Whale watching

- **Creating marine parks**
  - Some governments have created marine parks. These areas are protected by laws preventing pollution and controlling tourism.
  - The Great Barrier Reef in Australia is a marine park.

Great Barrier Reef, Australia

The white areas on this coral are damaged. This type of damage is called coral bleaching, and it is caused by an increase in sea temperatures.

- People now understand that pollution and **overfishing** are damaging the ocean. Laws are being made to protect this valuable **ecosystem**.

- Humans have explored only a small part of the oceans. There are still many discoveries waiting to be made.

Glossary

algae — simple plants that live in water

archaeologists — scientists who study the very distant past by looking at objects made long ago

bends — a medical condition caused by surfacing too quickly from a dive

cargo — goods that are transported for trade or sale

coral reef — structures made from the skeletons of tiny creatures called polyps

currents — systems of large amounts of water moving in a particular direction

decompression chamber — a room that slowly changes air pressure from the intense pressure under water to normal surface pressure, helping divers avoid the bends

dry suit — an insulated, waterproof suit that keeps a diver warm in cold waters

ecosystem — a particular environment where many varieties of plants and animals depend on each other to survive

equator — an imaginary line drawn around the middle of Earth that divides it into a southern half and a northern half

extinction — the result of a species of plant or animal dying out

gills — organs on a fish that take oxygen from the water flowing over them

icebergs — huge masses of ice floating in the sea

lure — something a predator uses to encourage prey to come closer

marine — relating to the sea

monsoon — a huge storm that occurs at a particular time each year in some Asian countries

nitrogen — a gas that is in the atmosphere and our bodies

nutrients — substances in food, soil, and water that feed animals and plants

overfishing — the catching of so many fish that the remaining fish do not have a chance to recover and reproduce

oxygen — a gas in the air and in water that most animals need to live

phytoplankton — a mass of plants that are so small that each one can only be seen with a microscope

pollution — harmful substances, such as dirt, waste, and chemicals, in the environment

rotation — the process of something, such as a planet, spinning in a circle

seabed — the floor of the ocean

seiners — boats used for fishing with a large net that hangs vertically in the water

sewage — waste matter carried by water

species — a category of living things or group of individuals sharing common traits

tides — the alternating rise and fall of the ocean's surface that happens about every twelve hours. The gravity of the Moon and Sun pulling on the water causes tides

trench — a long, very deep ditch in the ground or seabed

tropical — relating to the areas of the world near the equator

tsunamis — huge waves often caused by earthquakes or volcanoes erupting under the sea

zooplankton — a mass of very tiny animals

For Further Information

Books

Diving to a Deep-Sea Volcano. Scientists in the Field (series). Kenneth Mallory (Houghton Mifflin)

Explore the Ocean. Explore the Biomes (series). Kay Jackson (Capstone Press)

Ocean Habitats. Exploring Habitats (series). Paul Bennett (Gareth Stevens Publishing)

Tsunamis. Natural Disasters (series). Jil Fine (Children's Press)

Water on the Move. Cycles in Nature (series). Suzanne Slade (PowerKids Press)

Web Sites

Missouri Botanical Garden.
www.mbgnet.net/salt/oceans/index.htm
Click the links on the left to find out more about oceans.

Ocean World.
oceanworld.tamu.edu/index.html
Click on the pictures to find out more about the features of oceans.

Publisher's note to educators and parents: Our editors have carefully reviewed these Web sites to ensure that they are suitable for children. Many Web sites change frequently, however, and we cannot guarantee that a site's future contents will continue to meet our high standards of quality and educational value. Be advised that children should be closely supervised whenever they access the Internet.

Index